The Secrets of the Santa Muerte

Kenneth Bell

Published in 2016 by FeedARead.com Publishing

Copyright © Kenneth Bell

The author asserts his moral right under the Copyright, Designs and Patents Act, 1988, to be identified as the author of this work.

All Rights reserved. No part of this publication may be reproduced, copied, stored in a retrieval system, or transmitted, in any form or by any means, without the prior written consent of the copyright holder, nor be otherwise circulated in any form of binding or cover other than that in which it is published and without a similar condition being imposed on the subsequent purchaser.

A CIP catalogue record for this title is available from the British Library.

Dedication

I must begin by thanking the very many people in Mexico who gave up their time to talk to me about their beliefs and forms of worship.

In the United Kingdom, I want to give my thanks to Peter and Tim for their proofreading and editorial skills.

Finally, I need to thank the men that I used to sit around with in the bar of the Oxford Union back in the early-mid 1980s, and who are now, like me, a lot older and considerably fatter. We are spread all across the globe these days, but meet up virtually in a Facebook group, where their sardonic drollery provided me with much entertainment as I prepared the manuscript of this book for publication.

I invite all of these people to take what they wish from this short volume and count it as their own.

Needless to say, the errors are all mine.

Kenneth Bell
Edinburgh
21 February 2016

Contents

Introduction	Pg 1
1. A Brief History of Death	Pg 3
2. Worship	Pg 11
3. The Altar	Pg 15
4. Purifying the Altar	Pg 19
5. The Statuette	Pg 25
6. Incense	Pg 29
7. Simple Candle Rituals	Pg 31
8. Crystals	Pg 37
9. Offerings	Pg 41
10. Spells	Pg 45
11. The Seven Sacred Seals	Pg 57
12. The Symbolism of the Coconut	Pg 67
13. Some Final Thoughts	Pg 69

Introduction

If you have never heard of the new religion that is sweeping Mexico then you almost certainly will fairly soon. Not just because of the book that you are reading at the moment, but because the growth of the Santa Muerte religion has been nothing short of phenomenal.

From its beginnings in the early 1990s it had spread by 2010 as far north as California and as far south as Argentina. If a religion can do that in less than a generation, then crossing the Atlantic should pose no real problem. We can probably expect the first shrine to open in Great Britain any day.

What are the origins of this religion, and what factors led to its creation? How has it managed to spread itself so quickly? These are just some of the basic questions that we shall try to answer in the next section. Following on from that, we shall look at the mechanics of the religion, how the shrines are created in people's homes, and what is put on them. We will also, of course, look at some of the spells and incantations that the worshippers of the Santa Muerte use to invoke the supernatural entity.

Before we go any further, let us just mention the problem that any student of the Santa Muerte has, which is that little has been written about the religion in English; and, with one or two exceptions, most of what has been written seems to be poorly translated offerings from the original Spanish.

Thus, even the name is rendered incorrectly in English as Saint Death, but that is nothing more than a poor transliteration from the Spanish. A far better translation would be The Goddess of Death, and certainly she is worshipped in Mexico as a goddess in her own right. In researching this work the author has gone back to the few reliable sources that have been published in Mexico, but he has mainly relied on conversations with adherents of the Dark Lady. We need to remember that this is a folk religion, and as with all such belief systems, there are no hard and fast theological rules. People take aspects from other religions and add them to theirs with no thought for the poor scholar who is trying to untangle the knots that such practices create.

When in doubt, which has been most of the time, we have chosen the opinion that carries the most support, on the principle that there is wisdom in crowds. If that turns out to be incorrect then we hope that the Santa Muerte forgives us - if she exists, that is.

Chapter One

A Brief History of Death

Various claims have been made for the antiquity of the Santa Muerte cult. It has been claimed that it is a relic of pre-colonial times that somehow managed to remain a secret for five hundred years. Veracruz in the early Nineteenth Century is also put forward as a candidate. There it is said that a humble peasant saw the image of the Santa Muerte in the thatched roof of his house, an image that conveniently disappeared shortly thereafter. Finally, belief in the Santa Muerte is said to have originated in Hidalgo as late as 1965.

The problem that all of these claims have is a complete lack of proof. It may be argued that religions, by their very nature, require faith and not proof, but that is not the point. We have a fair idea of when Christianity was founded; surely we can do the same for the Mexican Death Goddess?

One thing is clear: when this writer moved to Mexico in 1990, the religion was unheard of by most people. On the 7th September 2001, a public shrine was inaugurated at Alfarera 12, in the Tepito district of Mexico City. Clearly, then, the cult's origins are prior to September 2001, but are unlikely to be very much earlier, otherwise its activities would have been noted.

What could have led to its creation? One factor is the relationship that Mexicans have long had with the whole concept of death. To the Western mind, death is something frightening that we prefer not to think about. The Mexican is just as frightened, but he is also willing to face death's reality, rather than try to pretend that it does not exist. Hence the Days of the Dead, on the 1st and 2nd of November every year. The Catholic Church likes to tell people that this is Mexico's version of All-Souls' Day, but actually that Catholic symbolism was overlaid atop a much older, purely Mexican, set of beliefs.

The Days of the Dead are so important to Mexican culture that any summary runs the risk of becoming a bowdlerisation, but we can say that these are the days when the spirits of the dead return to earth to commune with the living. On these days the children will pester their parents to buy them chocolate skulls. They also wander the streets dressed as ghostly figures clutching a hollowed-out pumpkin with a candle inside. It is probably from this tradition that the Americans acquired at least some of their Halloween customs.

A second factor must surely be the folk memories of the pre-Spanish gods that were formerly worshipped in Mexico. There were a lot of them, but the two that are of interest here are Mictlantecuhtli, the ruler of Mictlan, which is the place of the dead, and his wife and co-ruler, Mictecacihuatl. The god Mictlantecuhtli was always portrayed as a skeletal entity, and it is from him that the Day of the Dead symbolism grew to the chocolate and sugar skulls that children still eat in early November every year.

There are some adherents of the Santa Muerte who believe that their Dark Lady is the daughter of Mictlantecuhtli and Mictecacihuatl, who has been revealed to the people at this time to be their saviour and guardian. That is admittedly a minority belief amongst the Santa Muerte worshippers, but nevertheless the notion that the Death Goddess is directly descended from those older, Aztec entities is not all that uncommon in Mexico today.

Staying with the symbolism of the Santa Muerte for the moment, it is important to look at the people amongst whom the cult began. The Santa Muerte emerged amongst the *gentusa*, the common people of Mexico. Street traders, prostitutes, taxi drivers, policemen, and above all the drug dealers: it is there that we find the earliest worshippers of this new goddess.

All the literature refers to the drug dealers as being the most vociferous proponents of the Santa Muerte. They, and other members of the *gentusa*, are keen on body tattoos, and both Mictlantecuhtli and the Grim Reaper are favourite images. Is it too fanciful to suggest that someone took the Mexican way of treating death, added the tattoo imagery, and came up with the idea of the Santa Muerte? The creed was probably not fully formed in that way, but, pending further investigation, a tentative conclusion must be that its origins are to be found amongst those factors.

That the drug dealers popularised it is beyond doubt. Theirs is a dangerous world, with the threat of betrayal ever present. They are famous for their superstitions, and probably decided that having death, their ever present fear, on their side made sense.

This rather raises a question: why did a nascent creed amongst the urban *gentusa* spread so quickly? One can understand its attraction to drug dealers, but why are adherents to the cult now found amongst the ranks of the *gente decente*, the respectable class? Mexicans have always been a superstitious bunch, so that has not changed. Witchcraft of various kinds has long co-existed alongside mainstream Catholicism, but none of these beliefs ever grew into a new religion, still less one that could grow so quickly. Something must have happened in Mexico to make this growth possible.

The answer could be that what has changed in Mexico is the economy. Since 1988 the country has had a succession of Neo-Liberal governments who have opened the country up to outside forces. Globalisation, in other words, now affects Mexico as much as it does anywhere else. It is not just that the country is divided into rich and poor, *gentusa* and *gente decente*, because that has always been the case. Rather, it is that all the certainties that the old, closed economy provided now no longer apply. Given this, the Santa Muerte cult makes sense as a specifically Mexican response to changing circumstances. Put another way, the Santa Muerte may very well turn out to be a patriotic response to changes that many Mexicans see as being imposed upon their country from outside.

Staying on the theme of globalisation, aside from being responsible for the cult's birth, it may also have been responsible for its amazing growth. An idea that began in the slums has now spread throughout Mexican society and beyond its borders. That probably could not have happened without the Internet.

What the Internet did was to take a folk religion that existed without any rules or regulations, and one in which each adherent more or less created their own theology, and laid down its basic ground rules. The Internet is the Bible or Koran for the Santa Muerte, in other words, as well as its publicist.

This explains why the cult has now left its slum origins and is to be found amongst the ranks of the *gente decente*. The average upper-class housewife has no connection with her counterpart in the slums: unless we include conversation with the maids, cooks and nannies who work for her, that is. The Internet changed the rules of this game and allowed a slum cult to join the mainstream.

As belief in the Santa Muerte grew, the manufacturers of religious paraphernalia got in on the act. First to arrive were the statues of the goddess, obviously. Then the notion grew that the goddess could respond better to different appeals if her robes were of differing colours. Thus we now have red robes for love and amber for harmony. Luckily for the poor adherent to the cult, a black robed goddess gives total protection, so all areas are covered and at a reasonable price.

Next, someone began to manufacture special Santa Muerte lotion to ritually cleanse the statue before a ritual is performed. We also have Santa Muerte soap so that the practitioner can purify himself, as well as Santa Muerte incense that the purchaser is assured will please the goddess. Finally we now see the *dijes*, the small charm pendants that are worn around the neck or wrist, arriving on the scene.

So, to summarise, a set of religious beliefs began in the slums, and the small manufacturers of religious items got in on the act to cater for that. The Internet then publicised what was going on and helped set its rules. As more people found out about the Santa Muerte, yet more items related to it were produced to meet the growing demand. The cult grew, as it continues to grow to this day.

Interestingly enough, the Santa Muerte has become so strong that it has acquired a Catholic syncretism all of its own. The shrine that opened in 2001 is related to a group of Catholic traditionalists called the *Iglesia Católica Tradicional MX-USA, Misioneros del Sagrado Corazón y San Felipe de Jesús.*

These traditionalists registered themselves under Mexican law as a religious group that opposed the reforms of the Second Vatican Council. The problem is that they have now lost that registration because they spent most of their time arguing not in favour of the Latin Mass, but propounding the Santa Muerte idea. That is not to say that the Mexican government had suddenly decided to become a theological arbiter; rather the group fell foul of Mexican bureaucracy. They registered themselves to do one thing and then started doing another. The pen pushers just hate it when that happens, as it makes their files look even more untidy than usual.

Nevertheless, the traditionalists' presence has served to further publicise and promote the new religion. Its presence acts as a sort of half-way house for disaffected Catholics. They can plead favours from the Death Goddess, but at the same time, they do not have to make the full jump out of their Catholic faith.

Will this religion cross the Atlantic? It is hard to say with any certainty, but given that it now covers most of the Americas, it would be a foolish man who denied its possibilities in Europe. The very issues that led to its growth here are just as prevalent in the Old World: uncertainty about the future, unemployment, and the failure of the established religions to answer people's questions.

Of course, the Santa Muerte will never be as strong in the United Kingdom as it is in Mexico, but that is not the point. The UK is home to any number of pagan beliefs. It is quite likely that the Santa Muerte will take its place amongst them.

However, before that can happen, people need to know how the Death Goddess is worshipped, and that is something that we shall consider in the next chapter.

Chapter Two

Worship

For most Western people religion involves a sacred text, the Bible, which is unchanging, and, for Catholics especially, a priesthood who interpret that text authoritatively. The Santa Muerte religion does not work along those lines as there is no agreed text and no priesthood. The relationship between the goddess and her worshippers is a personal one, with the worshippers themselves devising all the rituals, and keeping those which work whilst what fails to have any effect is jettisoned.

Furthermore, what exists between the goddess and the individual worshipper owes more to the hustle of a marketplace than it does to the rarefied atmosphere of a British church. What is going on is the striking of bargains between the deity and her individual adherents, with the worshipper seeking favours in return for praises to the supernatural being.

Pagan religions have always operated in such informal ways. They are based on the notion that all the gods are in competition with each other for adherents. The gods do favours for men to show how powerful they are, and in return the humans then tell everyone just how much they have been helped by the all-powerful deity. Both sides gain from the deal, with the god getting more followers, thus climbing the league table vis-à-vis other supernatural beings, and the followers on Earth getting the goodies that they want.

How does this work in practice? Well, I remember that one day I turned up to meet my then lover, who inveigled me into driving her around

Mexico City because she just had to have a larger Santa Muerte statue than the relatively small one that then had pride of place in her main room.

I knew next to nothing about the Santa Muerte at the time, but I knew enough to drive her to the Sonora Market in Mexico City which is a centre for witchcraft and occult supplies of all kinds. It may be hard for a Westerner to believe, but Mexico City really does have its very own occult market where one can buy anything and everything related to the supernatural. As I battled the city's ferocious traffic, she explained that just before meeting me she had managed to get a Birkin handbag for herself from one of the city's more upmarket shops.

Looking at the bag which she held up triumphantly in front of her, it just looked like a large handbag to me, but being a man what could I be expected to know?

She explained at great length, and with much lip-smacking pauses as she delighted over her new possession, that these bags were not sold to all and sundry, and the fact that she had one would make her the envy of all her friends. As an aside she then told me that she planned to invite a dozen or so of her very best female friends to come around with a view to admiring her bag over coffee and cakes.

She then confessed that before going on her shopping expedition, she had made a promise to the Santa Muerte that if the shop would only give her exactly what her poor heart desired, then she would reward the goddess with a new, larger statue, one that would clearly dominate the room she was in.

We made it to the Sonora market and a large statue was purchased. The girl then spent the next hour or so, as I again fought my way through the traffic, cooing over her new handbag, stroking the new statue, and bending my ear about her good fortune to have discovered such a powerful deity who was so generous to her followers.

In a nutshell, everyone was happy. Well, except for me, as by then I could feel my enthusiasm for life ebbing away, but the girl got her bag, and the goddess received a new statue that was far bigger and grander than the old.

Reduced to an inner core, this is how pretty much all ancient religions operated, and how the Santa Muerte still does. The rituals are created by the adherents, and everything is done on the basis of a bargain between the god and the follower.

I might add that this is also how Catholicism operates as well. Back in the early 1990s I had a video shop in Mexico City which eventually I had to close. On the day that I shut the shop for the last time, more than one person told me that the reason for the failure was all due to the lack of a statue of Saint Matthew, who, as everyone knows, is the protector of small businesses. And there was me thinking that having to pay baksheesh to the police and the myriad municipal leeches had cut too deeply into the profits. Silly me, I suppose.

Today any number of books are being written to make money out of the gullible, by persuading them that the authors of these volumes are privy to the complicated secrets of the Santa Muerte's rituals. However, this writer believes that the old ways are the best, as do most of the followers of the Mexican Death Goddess come to that, so with that in mind the reader is advised to follow his or her own feelings when it comes to the rituals. There are a few hard and fast rules which we shall look at in the next chapter, but for the rest the readers should just do what seems right to them.

Chapter Three

The Altar

The altar is the essential part of the Santa Muerte belief, and if you decide to become a follower of the Dark Goddess then you will need to have one in your home where everyone can see it. It is the public proclamation of your devotion to the goddess, and it will form the centre of whatever rituals you adopt that are aimed at seeking her favours.

Many Mexican homes have a shelf along one wall or in the corner of a room, which serves as the family altar. However, many homes simply place a small table in a corner of the main room which serves as that family's altar, so there is no hard and fast rule other than that the altar should be in a prominent place.

Whatever you choose to have as the base for your altar needs to be covered in a white cloth of cotton or lace. This cloth should be spotlessly clean and freshly ironed.

In the centre of your altar you should place a statuette of the Santa Muerte or an image of the goddess. If neither is available then a single white rose in a stem vase is traditional. In fact, the white rose was the original symbol of the Santa Muerte cult before anyone thought to start manufacturing the statuettes, so by adopting this symbol you are reaching back to the origins of the belief; origins that would otherwise be lost in the mists of the late Twentieth Century.

Many people also have a large vase on their altar that has red roses or carnations in it. Red is the colour of blood, of course, but it is also represents the life forces of vitality, fertility and potency. Three red apples can also be used along with the flowers or in place of them.

On the subject of fruits, many altars also have a large banana on them as a symbol of male potency. Women who place them there are often seeking the goddess's help to fill an empty womb, either theirs or those that are carried by relatives.

A glass of water is found on just about every Santa Muerte altar to represent the basis of life itself. The glass should be spotlessly cleaned, and the water changed regularly. Many adherents drink the stale water, whereas others throw theirs away. There is no hard and fast rule on that, any more than there is with the disposal of fruit that has become over-ripe.

Bread is a common item found on altars, as this is the very staff of life. The rule here is not to throw away bread that has gone stale, but rather to crumble it up and throw it in a garden or other green spot.

Whatever you add or leave out of your altar, two items are found on almost every single Santa Muerte altar in Mexico. They are so important that this writer believes that they are just about the only items that cannot be excluded as they feature in so many rituals. Those items are alcohol and tobacco, with marijuana substituting for the tobacco if the practitioner prefers.

You should place a glass with your favourite drink in it on the altar. To be traditional, and Mexican, you might want to put out a glass of tequila or mescal, but I see no reason why a person in Scotland could not use a glass of whisky, or vodka for a Russian. Alternatively, a glass of your favourite wine would do the trick. If there is a rule, it seems to be to go with what makes you happy wherever you are in the world.

A packet of cigarettes or cigars, along with a clean ashtray, is also an essential part of the Santa Muerte altar. In fact, tobacco of some kind is the one item that most altars seem to have in common since virtually all the agreed rituals involve its use.

Substituting marijuana joints for regular cigarettes is something that people do for their more important rituals, when the need to commune with the Santa Muerte is all the more essential. This aspect of Santa Muerte rites is obviously something that is kept very private indeed, and I have never seen marijuana left out on an altar. Nevertheless, its use in the more important rituals cannot be denied, but whether you decide to adopt it for your Santa Muerte worship is a matter for you.

It must be accepted that the use of tobacco and alcohol - to say nothing of marijuana - makes the Santa Muerte a difficult goddess to follow for teetotal non-smokers who also have an aversion to mind-altering herbs, but anal retention is not something that the goddess encourages, so let's leave such people to follow Mrs Grundy rather than the Santa Muerte.

Quite why booze and smokes form such a basic part of Santa Muerte ritual is unclear, but they do. One explanation was given to this author by a female adherent who said that the Santa Muerte is *la cabrona*, and she appeals to *todos los cabrones en las calles*.

The word *cabron/cabrona* has many meanings in Spanish. In the sense that this woman used it she meant what the British call a hard arse. A street person who hustles for a living, selling this and that on street corners, or the police and city officials who take bribes off them.

Such people spend their lives in a cloud of tobacco smoke, on streets where the odour of cheap alcohol from the myriad cantinas hangs heavy in the air. Mixing their pleasures into their religion makes a kind of sense. Projecting those pleasures on to the Santa Muerte makes perfect sense, because it demonstrates that the Santa Muerte is at one with the *gentusa* and shares their earthy pleasures.

That said, the girl that I mentioned earlier who pestered me to drive her to the Sonora market to buy a large Santa Muerte statue was neither a drinker nor a smoker, although she did enjoy the odd joint from time to time, and she believes to this day that the goddess blesses her with favours.

Just don't be an anal retentive, and accept the rough-and-ready urban lifestyle of the people who have worshipped the Santa Muerte before you, and you will be fine in the arms of the Dark Goddess.

Chapter Four

Purifying the Altar

As I have said before there are no hard and fast rules about anything to do with the Santa Muerte, so what follows is a synthesis of the information that I obtained by talking to followers of the goddess in Mexico. The readers should feel free to adapt whatever they want from what follows, whilst ignoring the parts that do not suit them.

To purify your new altar you will need the following:

A small table.
A white cloth to cover it.
A statuette of the Santa Muerte, or a single white rose in a vase with water.
A bottle of your favourite alcohol.
A pack of cigarettes.
A glass or earthenware ashtray.
A large flower vase, filled with water, and a good bunch of flowers.
A glass of water and some fruits of your choice.
At least one white candle in a candlestick.
Incense of your choice, usually in a stick.

The purification of the altar is generally agreed to be the first ritual that a new follower of the Santa Muerte will perform. The consensus is that the ritual needs to be repeated nine times, on successive days, at more or less the same time and normally after darkness has fallen. With those factors in mind, you should choose your times and dates carefully to try and ensure that you are never disturbed during these important acts.

Before turning to the specifics of the altar purification ritual, we need to consider the ways in which you should purify yourself.

It is generally agreed that all major rituals should be carried out by a person who has first bathed or showered thoroughly. Clean yourself from head to toe, and while you are doing that, keep in mind the reason why you are doing it. You are about to approach a deity who is spiritually clean, so the act of bathing aims to put you on a similar plane to her. Perhaps needless to say, the act of allowing your mind to fix on the reasons why you are bathing will perhaps open the first link between you, the neophyte follower of the Santa Muerte, and the supreme being herself.

Once you are clean and dry, then dress yourself in freshly laundered, crisply ironed, clothing. Some people wear white, especially the ones who live in the Mexican coastal areas where the Santa Muerte has come into contact with the followers of the Afro-Caribbean Santeria religion. However, as always, there are no strict rules as to what you should wear, but everything you put on should be clean and worn in the name of the Dark Goddess.

Having bathed and dressed yourself, you can now proceed to lay out and then purify your new altar. You should do that in the style that is most agreeable to you, taking what follows merely as a guide to the consensus of opinion.

As you lay out the new altar you should quietly summon the goddess in your mind, telling her that this is in her honour, as a visible symbol of her powers, and in hope of the favours that she will grant you.

On the first day of your purification ritual, you should take a comfortable chair and sit down on it in front of the altar. Calm yourself totally and let your mind create the image of the Death Goddess as if she is right in front of you.

When you are ready, and when everything has been laid out to your complete satisfaction, then you should light your candle or candles, along with the incense. Allow a moment for the scent to permeate the room, and while it does that, you can switch off any electric lights that are still lit. You aim is to create a relaxed atmosphere with only the altar illuminated so that you can make it the centre of your concentration.

When you are ready, take the glass of spirits or wine that is on the altar in hand and salute the goddess with it. Hold it up so that she can see your tribute to her and, when your mind accepts that she is aware of the link between you, then take a deep swallow of the drink.

Return the glass to the altar and pick up the pack of cigarettes. You may then take one out and light it. When it is fully alight and has a nice glowing ember on it, place it on the ashtray with the butt facing the Santa Muerte statuette or white rose. Alternatively, you may simply place an unlit cigarette on the ashtray, but with the butt facing the Dark Goddess. Try not to touch the cigarette, or joint, until the ritual is over as it is what the Santa Muerte will symbolically smoke.

Take another cigarette and light it for yourself. Inhale the smoke deeply into your lungs and then blow it over the altar. You should do this nine times altogether, and after each exhalation you should speak a version of the following:

In your name, Mother Death, I implore you to grant me the favours that I seek. Grant them until the very moment that you summon me to your divine and eternal presence. Sacred Mother, do not deny me your protection, and in return I dedicate this altar in your name, that all men may see your power. So mote it be!

Having done all that you may leave the altar or do as most people seem to, which is sit back and reflect on the course of actions that you are taking. It is generally agreed that this reflection is helped enormously by the alcohol that might still be in the glass, so make sure that you pour yourself a decent belt before you begin.

When you are ready, put the remains of your cigarette in the ashtray along with the one that is for the Santa Muerte and then leave the candle to burn itself out in the fullness of time.

The following morning you should clear out the ashtray by scattering the ashes to the winds outside your door and tearing apart what remains of the two cigarettes before casting them to the winds as well, if they have both been lit. If you did not light the cigarette that was offered to the Santa Muerte then you may save it and use it yourself that evening, with a new one laid out for her. Whatever you choose to do with the cigarette, the altar then needs to be prepared again for that evening with a new candle, the ashtray thoroughly washed, and fresh alcohol in the glass.

As was said earlier, this ritual should be performed a total of nine times on successive evenings before the altar is properly sanctified. If at any time the ritual is interrupted or you are unable to carry it out on one evening, then you must start the whole process again from the first day. The followers of the Dark

Goddess believe that this interruption is a sign from the deity that you are not fully prepared to enter into her service, so you should wait a day or so and rededicate yourself to her in your mind before starting the purification ritual again.

Once the nine days are finally over then congratulations, as you are now an adept in the worship of the Santa Muerte. In fact, you could probably stop reading this slim volume right now because pretty much everything that most adherents agree on has already been said.

Many people use a shorter version of the purification ritual to summon the Dark Lady to the altar and create a link with her so that prayers and conjurations can be performed.

Each practitioner uses slightly different forms, of course, but a basic one would involve sitting at your altar, lighting your candles and incense sticks, before raising your glass to the Santa Muerte and drinking deeply from it. Then you might light a cigarette and blow smoke nine times over the altar as you call the Dark Lady in your mind.

Before we end this chapter let a word of warning be given. All the adepts who agreed to speak about their beliefs gave this warning, so passing it on to you makes perfect sense to this writer. Abandoning the Santa Muerte is quite acceptable if she does not give you the goodies that you want. The whole point about religion and the supernatural is to find yourself a powerful god, so if this one does not meet your requirements then you are perfectly at liberty to find another that does.

However, what you cannot do is continue to proclaim that you are a follower of the Santa Muerte and then fail to keep your side of the bargains that you make with her. If you fail to deliver on a pledge having received a favour from her then it is generally agreed that the consequences can be quite unpleasant, to put it mildly.

So unless you want the Mexican Death Goddess creating nightmares for you, or worse, then be warned to always keep to your side of the deals that you make with her.

Chapter Five

The Statuette

It is quite acceptable to use a white rose on your altar to represent the Santa Muerte, but most people now have a statuette of the goddess there instead. In Mexico every town will have at least one shop that sells them, along with incense and cards that contain Dark Goddess imagery.

Getting hold of a statuette for your altar in the United Kingdom is rather more difficult, but Amazon has them for sale as do other on-line retailers. You can also get in touch with me as I have a limited supply of statuettes, incense sticks and wallet-sized cards for sale. At the end of this book you will find more details of all that, along with my contact details, but for the moment let's concentrate on the symbolism that you will find in the statuettes.

The bulk of the statuettes have the Dark Goddess clothed in black. Turn the statuette over and look at the base and you will see that your new statue has been charged with seeds that have been moulded into the base. The seeds represent all the bounties that the goddess can bestow upon those who are faithful to her, such as wealth, happiness and fertility. Before leaving the small workshops where they are made, your statuette will have been blessed by a senior adept in the service of the Dark Goddess, and such a statuette is said to be fully charged with that person's powers.

Looking at the statuette, you might see some or all of the following: a scythe, a globe, an hourglass, a set of scales, an owl and a lamp. Let's look at each one in turn.

The scythe is usually held in one hand and represents the ability of the Santa Muerte to cut down negative energies and prevent them from reaching you. In addition, the scythe also represents the harvest, which is a time when people look forward to bounty and prosperity. In short the symbolism here is of protection and good fortune.

The globe is often held in the other hand. This represents the power that the Santa Muerte holds over the whole planet and its riches. By putting yourself under her protection, you can obtain some of those riches for yourself.

The hourglass you will often see in the robes of your statuette. It is a very old symbol, which was first used soon after the hourglass itself was created in the Alexandria of the Second Century AD, and here it represents the passage of a lifetime. It reminds us not that time flies, but that things happen in their own good time. So the symbolism here is one of patience and fortitude when faced with life's vicissitudes.

The scales represent justice, of course, under the beneficent wisdom of the Santa Muerte. By presenting the scales perfectly balanced, the imagery also denotes the peace and harmony that the Dark Goddess brings to her followers.

An owl is often seen near the feet of the Santa Muerte as a representative of wisdom. The imagery reminds us that we should open our minds to the new ideas that the Dark Goddess brings us, as well as looking ahead clearly.

The lamp represents not just the clarity with which you stride forward under the protection of this powerful being, but also the eternal nature of the light that she brings to the world. The light is eternal, as, of course, is the Santa Muerte. So you shall be eternal, because when you cease to live on this earthly plane then you will pass over to the after world where the light of the Santa Muerte shines all the brighter.

A final note needs to be added here. This imagery can be found on some statuettes, whereas other will have just a few and some none at all. It really depends on who made the statuette that you have bought.

Do not worry if your statuette does not have everything that I have described, because you can add them as extras to the altar if you wish. For instance I know of one Mexican Santa Muerte follower who inherited a statuette from her late mother. There was no globe, so my friend went and bought a large print of the earth as seen from space which she placed on the wall behind her altar. It actually looks rather nice and created just the imagery of the whole world under the Santa Muerte that my friend wanted to have in her home.

Many people who wish to concentrate on the wisdom and far-sightedness that the religion brings to its practitioners will buy a small statuette of an owl and then place it on their altar alongside the statuette of the Santa Muerte herself.

This is the nice thing about folk religions - you can add whatever you like to the imagery, in whatever way you like. If something works for you, then that is all that matters, as there is no thuggish, masculine priesthood telling you how you must worship.

Chapter Six

Incense

Incense has been used for many centuries in many religions, so it should come as no surprise that it has been taken up by the followers of the Santa Muerte. Aside from being pleasant, the fragrance acts to create the right mood, something which is very important in religions such as the Santa Muerte, since they rely on a personal link being created between the deity and the adherent. Followers of the Santa Muerte believe that the following five incenses are the core scents of their creed. Luckily for you, they are all available in the United Kingdom, either as raw incense or in stick form.

Copal: This resin from the copal tree has been used in Mexico as an incense for many centuries. The noun is actually a corruption of copalli, which is the name for incense in the Nahuatl language. Nahuatl, in case you are interested, was the lingua franca of Central Mexico prior to the Spanish conquest, and the official tongue of the Aztec Empire. Copal incense is what we may call the standard incense that is often seen on a Santa Muerte altar. More specifically it is used to clear the air of negative energy, to make the room more receptive to the presence of the Santa Muerte.

Myrrh: This is another ancient incense. According to tradition, it was one of the gifts that the three wise men brought to Bethlehem to give to the baby Jesus. In today's Santa Muerte it is used to prevent envy, intrigue or hatred entering the house.

Musk: Used as a barrier to disease or infirmity entering the house.

Sandalwood: This happens to be the writer's favourite scent of all, as a matter of fact. In Santa Muerte rituals it is used to attract prosperity or economic success to the adept.

Rose: Burned as an aphrodisiac, to attract someone and awaken their passions.

These, then, are the five main incenses of the Santa Muerte, but as with everything else connected to the Dark Lady, none of them is fixed and immutable. Some worshippers use church incense for all their rituals, whereas others create mixtures of their own. More than a few now buy the specially created Santa Muerte incense sticks which are on sale these days in the Mexican shops and markets that deal in the esoteric.

This being so, the advice here is to take the list of incenses that you have on this page and experiment with them and others to create the scents that appeal to you personally.

Incense is used to help put you in the correct frame of mind so that a link is created between you and your Dark Lady. If Musk, say, has more of an aphrodisiac aroma to your senses than Rose, then go with that which is more appealing to you.

Chapter Seven

Simple Candle Rituals

Rituals that involve lighted candles are very common with the followers of the Santa Muerte. Some people just light a candle and hope for the best, but many have turned to a more complicated rite to hopefully ensure that the Death Goddess takes notice of them.

You could start by sitting at your altar with a candle in your hand and then raise it in salute to the Dark One before placing it in its stick and lighting it in her name. As you do that, in your mind you should tell her simply and in your own words what you want and, crucially, tell her what she can get from you in return.

Remember that what all the gods want are more followers, so you could tell her that if she grants your wish then you will tell more people about her. That is the easiest and most usual bargain that people offer to the Santa Muerte.

You could add some of your favourite tipple to the mix if you wanted, by repeating part of the altar purification ritual that we looked at in the last chapter. Raise your glass to the goddess, and commune with her as you let the liquid flow down your throat.

There are seven colours of candle that you need to be aware of, and they are listed here along with their powers:

Black: This colour of candle can be burned to keep negative energies - as well as negative people - away from the adept. It is also used in rituals where the adept wishes to conjure up negative energies and then direct them at an enemy. One woman told me that she had burned a black candle and implored the Death

Goddess to injure a woman who had spirited my informant's husband away. She told me with great glee that the other woman had subsequently fallen down some stairs, so it seemed to work for her. She also told me that conjurations such as this are best performed with rather a lot of alcohol, in her case a bottle of red wine, and she stayed at the altar until it had all been consumed.

Blue: This colour is used for concentration and study, in theory. In practice it is almost always used by students who have done no work at all and who light it on the night before their exams. Needless to say, more than one lecturer will also be burning a black candle that night in the hope that black can defeat blue.

Brown: Used for health and to keep sickness at bay.

Gold: Perhaps obviously, this colour is related to money and wealth. The aim in lighting one is to open the road to success and prosperity.

Pink: This colour is used for love in the romantic or sentimental sense.

Red: This one is for passionate love or desire. It is lit to try and induce someone to have sex with the adept.

White: Finally, this is the standard, all-encompassing candle that will cover anything and everything. If you cannot get hold of a specific colour, then white will do instead. It is the original candle of the Santa Muerte, just as the single white rose was once her only symbol.

Understanding your candle light.

For obvious reasons your candle should not be in any draughts. Assuming that is the case, the Santa

Muerte adept will draw conclusions from the way that the candle flame behaves. The people that this writer spoke to in Mexico all advised that it is necessary to watch the flame for a few minutes to draw a correct conclusion, and avoid the possibility of reaching an erroneous one from an unexpected draught of wind.

The flame is normal:
If the flame burns normally, without any oscillation, and at a usual height, then the adept will conclude that the ritual is proceeding correctly and the desires that have led to it will be met eventually.

It is as if the Dark Goddess is telling you that she has heard your supplications and is willing to assist you if you only have faith in her powers. Many adepts will then redouble their efforts to achieve their ends, especially in the case of matters of the heart. The Santa Muerte is telling you that she is on your side, so push forward because your desires are on the cusp of being achieved.

The flame oscillates:
This is a tricky one, and first you must double check that there is no possibility of draughts entering the room to make the flame wave about. Assuming that this is the case, then the conclusion reached is that someone or something is interfering with your desires.

It could be that the person is yourself. Are you sure of what you are doing? Do you have total confidence in the Dark Goddess and her powers? If, having looked deeply into your own heart, you feel that the fault does not lie with you, then you must look to other people who are standing in the way of your achieving your aims.

It may be that the person that you want to attract is thinking about you constantly, but is unsure of their feelings. They may be influenced by other people who are acting against you, but something is troubling them when they think about you.

In the case of money matters, the oscillating flame tells you that someone is working against you. It could be that they do not wish to see you promoted at work, or are advising the person you approached for a loan not to give it to you.

To be forewarned is to be forearmed in cases like this, so at least you know that the Santa Muerte is on your side and is telling you to be careful. It is possible, of course, that you already had an inkling of who the opposition actually is, and now your Dark Goddess is confirming the truth of what you already suspected.

You may now proceed with more confidence, secure in the knowledge that she is on your side.

The flame leans to the right:

If the flame tends to the right then you should conclude that this is a positive sign of stability for you and your family. Nothing out of the ordinary can be expected in the short term, and matters will proceed on their usual course.

The flame leans to the left:

This is a warning that for whatever reason the time is not right to continue along your chosen path. You should reassess your chosen strategy and try to find a new approach to your aims. Once you have done that, then you should start the ritual again to see if you get a different sign from the Santa Muerte. One thing is clear: if you persist in the current way then you are unlikely to get what you want.

The candle jar breaks:
Many people use candles in glass jars, since they help to prevent draughts from interfering with the meanings that the flames seek to convey. If the glass breaks of its own accord on the altar, then the meaning is that someone very close to you, possibly the person that you least expect, is working against you. It could be that they are using magic of their own against you, so keep your top eye open and be careful who you trust.

The flame is very small:
This is a sign that your petition will take a long time to reach its fruition, but that the result will be pleasing to you when it arrives. Take your time and whatever you seek will be yours, but over rather a longer time-scale than you expected when you began.

The flame is long and bright:
This is the sign that everyone dreams about getting. It means that your desires are within reach and will be fulfilled very, very shortly.

The flame is flickering:
The bad news here is that you will not get everything that you want, but the good news is that you will get some of your heart's desires. The Dark Goddess is telling you that half a loaf is better than none.

The flame is unstable and constantly rises and falls:

This is a sign from the Santa Muerte that you are unsure as to what you really want. You should take the time to reassess your desires and decide if they are really that important for you.

The flame goes out of its own accord on more than one occasion:
This can have two meanings:
The first is that although your desires will be met eventually, you are surrounded by the negative energy of people around you who dislike you.

The second might indicate that you or someone close to you is about to become very ill.

One piece of advice that I was given by more than one follower of the Santa Muerte is worth passing on to the reader here. It is that your ability to interpret the meanings that are being conveyed to you by the candles will improve as time goes by. In the beginning you will confuse one signal with another, and thus draw conclusions that the passage of time will show you to have been just plain wrong.

That does not mean that the Santa Muerte is wrong. It simply means that your skills at interpreting what she is saying to you are not yet fully developed.

So the watchword here is one of patience. As a neophyte your link to the Dark Lady is going to be weak and tenuous. As you improve in your understanding of the rituals your link to her will strengthen and her meanings will become all the clearer.

Chapter Eight

Crystals

The magical potency of crystals has been known for centuries in Mexico and these multicoloured stones are used in all types of traditional religious practices throughout the country. Before looking at the different colours and their uses, let us spend a moment to consider what you need to do when you are buying your supplies.

Followers of the Santa Muerte all say that you should look for crystals that seem to be speaking to you. Hold them in your hand and see how they feel. Equally as importantly, how do you feel as you hold the individual crystal in your hand? If you feel comfortable with it, then spend a moment to tell your Dark Goddess that you wish to buy the crystal in her name. If you still feel comfortable with the piece in your hand, then you should know that the Dark Lady has welcomed your choice.

Every crystal that you own is used as a kind of booster to increase the link that already exists between your deep, subconscious mind and the Santa Muerte. They do not create that link - that comes from you - but they do act to strengthen it. That is why people have used them down the centuries.

In a moment we shall look at the different colours and the powers that each one contains within it, but for the moment let us look at how a crystal is used to strengthen your link to the deity.

You might prepare your altar in the usual way. Light a candle, and, if you wish, use the ritual of alcohol and tobacco to commune with the Dark Lady.

Then, when you are ready, take your crystal and hold it up so that she can see it. Hold it there and with all the power that your imagination can summon imagine that she is nodding with approval at your actions.

Once the spiritual link has been created, you can strengthen it by holding the crystal cupped in both hands and imagining that your petition to the Santa Muerte is travelling through the crystal. It is as if the object in your hand is magnifying the sounds from your deep mind, sounds that only you and she can hear.

Keep repeating your desire until you are satisfied that the words have been heard on the other side. Then, when you are totally satisfied, place the crystal gently on the altar and leave it there for several days. The potency that is inherent in the crystal will continue to commune with the Santa Muerte in your absence, and the powers of the Dark Goddess will flow from her into the crystal, thus increasing its overall powers and effectiveness.

You may then carry the crystal in your pocket or handbag, but try to make sure that nobody else touches it. The powers that are contained within that small object are for you and you alone.

Crystals and small stones each contain two powers within them. The first is to remove bad energies and the second is to aid in the obtaining of something. The colours, with their respective powers are as follows:

Black: This rock eliminates anger and helps to create peace and harmony.

Blue: Will block evil sensations and encourage your intuition and connection with the spiritual world.

Green: This colour is ideal for preventing insecurity and inner tension, as well as helping you to feel at peace, with an inner tranquillity.

Orange: An ideal piece to ward off self-doubt and insecurity. It is ideal for encouraging your creativity.

Pink: Will eliminate love problems and increase your sense of romance.

Red: Prevents uncertainty and weakness, whilst encouraging passions of the wilder kinds such as lust.

Turquoise: This is perfect for warding off the evil eye and helps to prevent all other kinds of witchcraft that are directed against you. It encourages your inner strengths, such as fortitude and self-worth.

Violet: Acts to prevent uncertainty and sadness, whilst boosting your inner tranquillity and harmony.

White: This will prevent other people's anger from harming you, and help you to create a feeling of inner peace and harmony within yourself.

Yellow: Acts to block negative energies of all kinds, as well as encouraging a clearness of thought and the ability to analyse a situation.

In Mexico the use of crystals is encouraged for the neophyte practitioner as they are believed to carry a power that is intrinsic to them. Thus many people believe that a good crystal can almost speak to the person who is holding it.

Unlike the candle rituals which we looked at before, a crystal cannot be misinterpreted by the newcomer to the Santa Muerte and her rites. If it feels good in the hand, if you don't want to let go of it and absolutely have to own it, then that particular crystal will work for you.

Chapter Nine

Offerings

Perhaps the easiest way to persuade the Santa Muerte to give you what your heart desires is via an offering to her as part of a prayer. Such practices are fairly common in the established religions, but there is a slight difference in how they work with this deity.

Basically, you do not make an offering to the Santa Muerte; instead, what you do is tell her that she will get one if she grants you the favours that you seek. Of course you can give her a little taster of the main offering that will be hers once you have got what you want, so a small bunch of flowers could be left on the altar to whet her appetite for more and excite her interest in doing what, to the Santa Muerte, must seem like a small favour indeed.

The point that you must make it clear to her, via that magical link that you have created in your mind between the two of you, is that a very nice offering will go on the altar as a reward for doing you the service.

Once you have received your favour, then the clock starts to tick because you do not have much time to go out and buy the main offering to put on your altar. Remember, you do not want a cheesed-off Mexican Death Goddess getting irritated with you, so keep your side of the deal as quickly as possible.

The offerings that you should make will be ones that make the altar look grander and more imposing. Flowers are the obvious choice, with pinks for romantic love, heavily scented red roses for the more basic, lustier passions, and whites for health and well-being.

A barren woman will often put a single banana - the largest she can find - on the altar along with two large red apples. The symbolism of this is obvious and if her womb then acquires a tenant she will keep placing yet more fruit on the altar to ripen, and then eat it in the Dark Goddess's name throughout her pregnancy.

As you can see, what you place on the altar as your reward to the Lady of the Shadows as a reward for favours that you have received is really only restricted by your imagination. If you think about it, it is highly unlikely that a powerful entity like the Santa Muerte really cares all that much about the nature of the offering, but there are two factors at work here, which make the offering, whatever it is, very important indeed.

The first is that it shows that you can be trusted with the Santa Muerte's grace. You keep your side of the bargain and the evidence for that is right there on your altar. You are a trustworthy human that the goddess will smile on in the future, unlike the other poor wretches who forgot their side of the deal and now find their dreams tormented by demons sent to teach them a lesson in good manners.

Secondly, and even more importantly, you need to remember that this entity is very much the new kid on the block in the spiritual world. As we said earlier, all the gods are in competition with each other for followers because the more followers a god has the stronger he or she is in the spiritual league tables.

If you decorate your altar with a large bunch of heavily scented flowers, then visitors to your house will notice the altar and start asking you questions about it. You will obviously tell them about the good fortune that has come your way courtesy of the Santa Muerte, and, quite probably, they will take an interest in her themselves. It is not improbable to suggest that they may become worshippers themselves, and thus the Santa Muerte's position in the supernatural pecking order is strengthened over her rivals for the affections of human beings.

An offering on the altar is the simplest way of tempting the Dark Lady into bestowing her favours upon you, and for that reason it is particularly recommended to the new worshipper. That said, you can use other types of offering as well, since you are only restricted by your imagination.

One man I know suddenly started sporting a large, ostentatious, solid-silver belt buckle which he wore every day. He explained to me that it was his offering to the Santa Muerte in return for a favour received, so you really can let your imagination rip when it comes to a decent offering to your new goddess.

Funnily enough, in the crime-ridden urban jungle that is Mexico City, where violent street crimes are a daily occurrence, nobody ever tried to take that expensive item away from him.

Even the most desperate, drug-fuelled mugger is afraid to mess with the Dark Lady of the Shadows.

Chapter Ten

Spells

The difference between a spell and the prayers that we have already looked at is fairly simple. A prayer to a deity gives the supernatural being the option of refusing to help the supplicant. The followers of the Santa Muerte try to get around that by offering what amounts to a bribe to their Dark Goddess, but she can still decline the plea. With a spell the supernatural being has been bound to help by the nature of the conjuration and has no choice in the matter.

The spells which follow were collected by this writer on his last trip to Mexico in early 2015. Most practitioners of the occult keep their most powerful spells as closely guarded secrets, but the ones that I am about to give to you here are fairly well known, and I was able to check their veracity with several different practitioners.

Perhaps needless to say, all the versions that I was given differed slightly from each other, but that only reflects the folk nature of the Santa Muerte creed. There is no higher authority that anybody can appeal to in the case of a dispute, so each practitioner uses the forms that he or she feels the most comfortable with. That is as it should be, and on that basis all these spells reflect the consensus view of the Mexican practitioners who kindly agreed to share them with me.

One final point before we begin. Mexican witchcraft practitioners tend to end their conjurations with the words "Así sea," which translates roughly as "So it will be." I prefer to use the British way of ending an occult charge, so I have rendered the Spanish words as "So mote it be," a form of words that will be very familiar to anyone coming to the Santa Muerte from any branch of British witchcraft.

A spell to assist with legal problems:
You will need:
3 green candles
1 needle that has as not been used for anything other than the Santa Muerte rituals.
1 large sheet of green paper
1 pen with black ink or a pencil.

Again, try to use pens or pencils that are dedicated to the Santa Muerte rather than everyday items.

Begin as you always should by preparing yourself mentally for the task ahead by sitting at your altar and creating the magical link between the Santa Muerte and yourself in your own mind.

When you are fully prepared, write the name of the person who is due in court on the three candles using the needle. Then place each candle in its stick.

Take the sheet of paper and at the top you should sketch an image of the Santa Muerte. Do not worry about how bad it looks, what matters is that you have created it. If you really cannot draw to save your life, just do your best to sketch the deity's skull face, no matter how simple and cartoon-like it appears. Don't worry, nobody will see it.

Underneath the sketch you should write the name of the accused, the court that they will be tried in and the offence that you want them to be acquitted of. You can add as much or as little detail as you like, but while you are writing try to keep in your mind that this message will go straight to the Santa Muerte herself via the nature of the spell that you are casting.

When you have finished writing, allow yourself a moment to collect your senses. Hopefully the more flustered you are at that moment the better, because it means that your senses have been heightened, and thus the message is more likely to be received and understood on the other side.

When you are ready, place the paper face up in the centre of your altar and put your Santa Muerte statuette on top of it. Place a candle on either side of the statuette, and one in front. Then light each of the candles in turn.

Take a few moments to consider the way that the candles are burning. Do the three lights look as if a message is being sent to you and if so is it propitious to continue?

If you decide that it is, then rise to your feet and stand to your full height with your arms outstretched on either side, and the palms facing the altar.

You should then speak a version of the following charge. Your own words are better, so what follows is given only as a guide:

Dark Mother of us all: I charge by the powers of these lights that the road to freedom for me (or the name of the person concerned) be clear and illuminated. I charge that all enemies of the light cease to persecute me (or the person concerned). Great Mother, hear these words. So mote it be.

You should repeat, repeat and repeat again your charge, and the more hysterical and out of control you become during that process the better the result should be.

Finally, and hopefully when you are dripping in sweat and with tears rolling down your cheeks, you may collapse into your chair to collect yourself again.

When you are able, you may then leave the room, and the candles should be allowed to burn out of their own accord.

On the morning of the trial, remove the paper from the altar and fold it up. Take it with you to court and hopefully your desires will be granted.

A spell to increase your wealth:
You will need:
13 coins
A small handful of mustard seeds
Sandalwood incense
1 gold-coloured candle
1 dinner plate
A piece of card or paper, small enough to fit on the plate
A pencil or pen

Begin by lighting your candle and the incense stick.

Now sketch an image of the Santa Muerte on the paper, just as was done in the previous spell. Again, I don't want to keep repeating this for fear of boring you, but it is important that you understand that it really does not matter how bad your drawing talents are, just so long as you do the sketch.

When you have completed your sketch put it face up in the middle of the plate.

Now place twelve of the coins in a circle around the rim of the plate, and the final coin in the middle on top of the sketch.

Take your mustard seeds and sprinkle them in a circle around the coin that is in the middle of the plate.

Then announce in your own words that this conjuration is about increasing your wealth. When you have done that you should light the candle and spend some time considering the flame to decide if the moment is right to continue.

Finally, you need to complete the ritual with a charge of your own devising. Stand up straight, arms outstretched, with your palms facing the Dark Goddess. Take a deep breath and recite with all the intensity that you can manage something like:

Dark Mother of us all: you know what I need, and I call upon your powers so that the coins on this altar will multiply every day, and that the seeds will protect me as I go about my business in your name. So mote it be!

Again to repeat what was said in the first spell, you should keep repeating your charge time and time again until you are mentally and physically drained.

At the end, leave the candle to burn out of its own accord, and take the coins back into your pocket or purse. You can spend them, because they do not need to be saved, as they have served their purpose, but it is important that you take possession of them from the altar.

Collect the seeds and place them to one side on the altar, and then burn the paper with the Santa Muerte sketch on it. You can do that on the plate if it is safe to do that indoors.

Finally mix the seeds with the ashes of the paper and then sprinkle them in the doorways to your house. Some people also sprinkle some seeds in their place of business. This writer knows of at least one prostitute who seeks customers by standing on a particular street corner along Tlalpan in Mexico City. She sprinkles seeds around that corner and swears that the ritual brings in a better, more free-spending type of punter, as well as keeping the competition at bay!

A spell to help cure sickness:
You will need:
A good sized flower vase with water in it.
9 white carnations
Musk incense
A white candle
Light the candle and the incense stick.

Put the vase in the middle of your altar and then put the flowers one by one into the vase. As you do this, keep repeating a charge in your own mind that those flowers will draw from the Santa Muerte her healing powers, and those powers will be held by the flowers.

Spend a moment to consider the candle flame and see what it is telling you.

Take the flowers in one hand and then go to the room where the sick person is to be found. Gently stroke them from head to toe with the flowers, being careful not to damage the petals, if possible. As you do that you should imagine the power of the Santa Muerte that you have captured in the flowers flowing out to help the sick person's recovery.

Finally, return the flowers to their vase on the altar and leave them there to live out their lives. When the flowers die, you should remove them from the vase and take them for disposal as far away from the house as possible.

To help a woman recover her lost husband or lover:

You will need:
A pink candle for romantic love or a red one for the more passionate kind.
A pink crystal
Rose incense
A needle
A sheet of plain paper, preferably the same colour as your candle.
A pen or pencil.
A large plate

This is a silent conjuration, which for some reason is only used by women. That is not to say that a man cannot try it, but I have never heard of a man who has used it at all.

Sitting at your altar, you must begin igniting the incense and then silently telling the Santa Muerte why you are calling her. In this case it is about your wandering man, so tell her in your own way that you are calling up her powers over all men to ensure that yours returns to you.

Take as much time as you wish, and try to ensure that your sense of outrage or anger at your treatment reaches its full measure. You should not allow yourself to cry under any circumstances, as this is a ritual that involves your taking control of your man, but you do need to ensure that those other emotional senses are heightened to their fullest extent. If you can reach a stage that can really only be described as cold fury, then so much the better.

Light your candle and study the flame. If the omens seem good, then proceed to the next step.

On the paper you should create your Santa Muerte sketch, and then write the man's name and an instruction to return to you. Please note that you are not begging either him or the Dark Goddess here, so make sure that your words are clear and authoritative.

In the name of the Blessed Santa Muerte, I command you, John Smith, to return to me, Jane Jones. So mote it be!

You can use whatever form of words you wish, just so long as they are clear, concise and authoritative. In your mind you need to be clear that the weeping is over and this is about you taking powers from the Santa Muerte to use against your unreasonable man and bring him to heel.

Next place the paper on the plate, and put your Santa Muerte statuette on top of it.

When you have done that you can allow your senses to heighten to improve the potency of this spell. However, and to repeat, you must not allow yourself to become weepy under any circumstances. Instead remind yourself that you are not responsible for this situation, as the fault lies with him. For your part you love him in spite of his failings towards you.

When you feel that the charge has been fully applied, you may remove the statuette from the paper and then burn the paper to ashes on the altar. Collect the ashes in a small plastic bag and guard them carefully.

Finally, you need to arrange to see the man who has caused all the trouble. Make sure you dress in a way that delights you and hopefully him, and then meet him at the arranged place.

You need to sit upright and try to let him do the talking. As he tells you whatever nonsense comes into his head, encourage the babble with slight inclinations of your head.

Reach into your pocket or handbag and stick your thumb into the bag that has the ashes in. Then reach forward as if it is the most natural thing in the world and gently brush the collar of his shirt with your hand so that your thumb leaves a slight smear from the ashes on his clothing. If you can manage to do the same thing with his neck, so much the better.

Try to take his hands and leave an ash smear on the inside of both his wrists, but be careful that he doesn't catch you out, otherwise the spell will be broken.

When you have done enough ash marking, you can then interrupt his talk and tell him that you have heard enough. Quietly and firmly, with the powers of the Santa Muerte flowing through you, tell him why you are far more valuable and worthy that the odious little trollop that he is hanging out with, and then get up. As you walk away tell him to call you soon. That speech should last for no more than a minute at the most. Do not give him time to respond, just get out of there and leave him to brood and the Santa Muerte to do her work.

Those of you who are reaching out to the Santa Muerte from the British witchcraft tradition will probably recognise some or all of these spells as being variants of those that are used in your existing rituals. If that shows anything it is that there is little that is new in the world of magic. It may be that the Santa Muerte is actually a Mexican version of Hertha, the ancient Germanic mother goddess who arrived in Britain with the Saxon tribes.

If that is the case then this writer sees no reason why other aspects of the British craft cannot be taken on board by those who wish to worship the Mexican entity in Britain. Most supernatural practices and beliefs are syncretised fusions from other creeds, so it would be difficult to argue why the Santa Muerte should be in any way different.

Finally, the point needs to be made again that the rituals that surround the Santa Muerte are still in the process of being created. Since there is no priesthood to tell practitioners what they must believe, then adopting aspects from other creeds strikes this writer as being perfectly acceptable. All that matters is that whatever you take, be it from this book or from others, works for you.

For instance, in Mexico more than a few followers of the Dark Goddess use Catholic imagery that had been first adopted by the local witchcraft tradition in that country. Indeed, there are some spells, which the writer recognised as coming from that tradition, where the powers of Jesus Christ and the Santa Muerte are invoked in rituals that the Santa Muerte practitioners have clearly borrowed from the older, folk-religion version of Roman Catholicism.

One very popular conjuration that has switched from one to the other is a spell that aims to ensure that a man who has abandoned his woman and children at least pays something towards their upkeep.

The Catholic version involves an image or statuette of Christ, a banknote from the man's wallet which he should have been inveigled into lending, and a candle that has his name marked on it with a needle. The Santa Muerte option just replaces Christ with the Dark Goddess, and allows the woman to take the money from the man's wallet when he is in a drunken stupor. The candle is still engraved with his name, by the way.

Having lit the candle, the charge used by both sets of practitioners is virtually identical. The Catholic one demands that Christ throw off his guise of a lamb and appear as a roaring lion to avenge the humiliation of the supplicant; that the money she has placed in front of the burning candle will grow ten-fold as the man is forced by the mighty powers invoked to pay his due debts to the woman he has abandoned.

The Santa Muerte version drops the imagery of the lamb, and instead calls upon the Santa Muerte to put aside her caring, motherly aspect to appear as a vengeful wrath, but from then on the forms of words are basically the same.

Of course, all the practitioners say something that is slightly different, since all the invocations are created by the individuals themselves, so there is no need to present full translations here. What matters is that the people of both traditions are drawing from each other as they seek the supernatural powers that men and women have always sought to harness for their own ends.

This being so, it is unlikely that anyone can object if you take whatever you want from existing British traditions of witchcraft and magic, and then fuse them with the Mexican deity. If they work for you then tell people about it, and help spread the word of the Santa Muerte's coming to the people of Britain.

So mote it be, as the saying goes.

Chapter Eleven

The Seven Sacred Seals

The Seven Sacred Seals are used to contact the dead, protect against evil magic, increase wealth, obtain justice, seek knowledge, obtain love and increase personal power. Today they are widely considered to be the centrepiece of the Santa Muerte arts, and more than a few followers of the Santa Muerte use the Seven Sacred Seals for almost all their rituals.

So popular have they become that books have been printed that give professionally produced versions of the seals, and those designs are now readily available on the Internet. Just type the Spanish words *siete sellos sagrados santa muerte* into Google if you do not believe me, and there you will find them, along with instructions as to their use.

If you wish, you can download any or all of those Internet versions and use them instead of the versions that you will find in this book. If you wish to do that, then just remember that you should print the image of the seal that you need and then write your petition on the other side of the paper. After that the ritual is pretty much the same as the version that you will find here in a moment.

Before the seals became commercialised, the followers of the Dark Lady created their own, and many believe that only by adding their own talents to the mix - however humble they may be - can success really be assured. Indeed, most of the Spanish-language books and sites which offer these seals will invariably tell the practitioner to leave the seal on the altar for two full days so that it can charge with the powers of the Santa

Muerte. This is not the case if you create your own seal, as the act of drawing it yourself, at the altar and in the Santa Muerte's name, will charge the seal automatically.

To create a seal, you need to take a sheet of plain white paper. If the paper is A4 size, then fold it in half to make A5, and if you wish you can fold it again to make an A6 booklet.

Sitting at your altar, having made what has now become your usual method of contacting the Dark One, you should take a pair of compasses, or something as simple as a cup, and draw a circle on the front cover of your folded paper. Then do the same on what is, in effect, the back cover. The seals will be slightly different for each power, but they are all created within those circles, one on the front and an identical one on the back. Open the paper out once, so what was folded as A6 becomes A5, and that is the space where you should write your petition.

Let's now look at each seal in turn and show how they are created:

To contact the dead:

This is the easiest seal to create since all you need to do is draw images of the Santa Muerte within your two circles. Remember that a basic skull will do, just so long as you believe with all your heart that the image that you create is truly that of the Dark One herself. Other seals will need more imagery to assist their potency, but this one calls to the Santa Muerte in her basic power as mistress of the underworld, so it needs no further elaboration.

Open your paper out just once if you have double-folded it, and on the left hand side you should write the name of the deceased you wish to contact, and their dates of birth and death. On the other side of the paper you will then write the questions that you have for them.

Please note that the questions especially should be written in red ink. The imagery on the front covers can be created in pencil, but all sources agree that the questions need to be written in red. Given that this is the easiest seal to create, but also the most difficult to have success with, then you might feel obliged to follow this advice to the letter.

Having done that, you should place the newly created seal on the altar and sit there for a time yourself to collect your thoughts. Many people take the opportunity with this ritual to take an extra large amount of whatever alcoholic drink they use in their rituals, and those who use marijuana as part of theirs almost always roll an extra-large joint.

Finally, when you feel that the time is right and that full communion with the Dark Lady has been achieved, you should take the seal in both hands, hold it against your breast and utter your version of the following words:

Mother of us all: by the power of this seal that is sacred to you, I entreat you to allow (Name of deceased) to leave your presence in the world where you reign supreme, to answer my questions. So mote it be!

If you can repeat the charge time and time again until you build yourself up into a crescendo of power then so much the better. This is a ritual that certainly needs it because summoning the dead is one of the most difficult rites to perform, so you really need to let your emotional juices flow. Needless to say, the alcohol will help with this, so don't stint on its use that night.

Finally, when you are utterly drained, you may leave the altar, with the seal on it.

When you go to bed, which should not be long after the ritual has been completed, take the seal with you and sleep with it under your pillow. If all went well with the ritual then the dead person will visit you in your dreams and answer your questions.

If you wake up in the morning with all your questions answered, then you must immediately return to the altar to thank the Santa Muerte. You should also place the seal on a plate at the altar and burn it to ashes.

If the ritual has failed - and for many people it will, as getting the Santa Muerte to release any of her children even for a moment is difficult - then the seal still needs to be burned, and a fresh one created should you decide to try the ritual again another night.

Protection against evil magic:

This conjuration is simple to perform and is very popular in Mexico, with the adherents of the Santa Muerte claiming that it will protect the user against all types of malicious witchcraft, including Voodoo and Santeria.

The seal should be created as soon as you feel that someone is using the dark arts against you.

Create your seal by folding the paper in the usual way, adding the circles and then sketching your Santa Muerte image within the two circles. You should leave space below the Santa Muerte so that you can add a drawing of a scythe. This represents the power of the Santa Muerte to cut through evil in all its forms.

On the inside of the seal you should state simply what you feel are the symptoms of the spell that has been cast against you. If you wish, you can also name the person who you feel is acting against you, but that is not a necessary part of the ritual.

Now hold the seal in both hands and press it to your breast, holding it there while you utter your version of the following summons:

Santa Muerte, I invoke you to my presence and command you to take your scythe and cut down all spells and conjurations that have been cast against me. Do this for your faithful servant and I will make an offering in your name that will please you. So mote it be!

That's it! Short, simple and never known to fail. Let's be honest, what supernatural entity wouldn't want to come along and prove just how effective they are at getting rid of competitor beings? To make matters even nicer, you have offered the Santa Muerte a nice sweetener in the form of a future offering that will go on your altar.

You can now burn the seal on your altar, secure in the knowledge that the hex against you has been broken.

Finally, do not forget the offering. At the very least, the Dark Lady deserves a big bunch of flowers, don't you think?

To increase good fortune:

This conjuration aims at increasing the adept's good fortune, mainly in the financial sense. That is not to say that it will help you to win the lottery, but it is believed to help in the more general sense of helping an adept to obtain a new job that pays more money, or even to get a job after a period of unemployment.

The seal is created in the usual way, and the adept should then add symbols of wealth to it. One way to do that is to take a coin and draw around it, and perhaps then add the "£" symbol for the British pound, or the "$" for the dollar.

Then using brown or violet ink, you should state briefly inside the seal what it is exactly that you want. The new job, any job, a loan, good luck at work - Mexican beggars have been known to use this conjuration before they hit the streets with their hands outstretched, so it can be used for anything that aims to increase a person's luck in obtaining wealth, in whatever way.

Having created your seal, it should then be held in both hands over the breast in the usual way as you utter a conjuration such as this:

Sacred Mother: I invoke you with the power of this sacred seal that has been created in your name. I command the powers within it to pass to me, so that the fortune that I seek shall be mine. So mote it be!

The seal may be left on the altar overnight, and should be burned the next day.

To obtain justice:

The symbol for justice in the Santa Muerte rite is a set of scales, so you need to sketch one underneath your drawing of the goddess. A simple large letter "T" will do with two cups shown dangling from the arms of the crosspiece.

You should then set out your case in simple terms using black ink inside the seal. You can be as honest as you want with this seal since justice, to the

Santa Muerte adept, is defined as getting the results that he or she wants from the courts or police.

The conjuration might go something like this:

Holy Mother: I place my case in the balance of your scales, that justice will be mine as a true believer in your sacred rites. I call upon you to free me (or the person that you name) from these charges, that I may further exalt your holy name. So mote it be!

This seal should then be burned at once, something which is especially important if you are confessing that you actually carried out the actions that have led the court to take an interest in you!

To obtain knowledge and wisdom:

This seal is often used when an adept has to make a critical decision and is uncertain as to the correct path down which to proceed. The aim of the seal is to heighten our powers of analysis, while at the same time keeping us calm so that we can behave rationally as we consider our options.

Perhaps needless to say, it is also used by students who find themselves facing an examination for which they have done little or no work.

The seal is one of the trickier ones to produce, since the Santa Muerte rites use the image of an owl as the sign of knowledge, which means that you will have to sketch an owl in the circle underneath your Santa Muerte drawing.

So long as whatever you produce looks like an owl in your mind, or you can be persuaded to accept that it represents that particular bird, then you should be fine. On the other hand, if you cannot accept that your attempt is anything other than a squiggle, you could pay a visit to Google and look up the clip art that features owls. You should find something there that you can print off and then trace onto your seal. It would mean using tracing paper for the actual seal, but at least it would give you the necessary imagery.

Having designed the seal, you should write your petition inside using black ink. Set out your problem clearly, and write down the options that you feel that you have. Take your time with this aspect, and imagine that the Santa Muerte is looking down on you as your pen works its way across the paper.

When you have finished, fold the seal, and then recite your version of the following with the seal clasped to your breast in both hands:

Santa Muerte: I call upon you to bless me with your infinite wisdom, that an answer may be found. Guide me towards your light, and allow me to receive the gift of your infinite wisdom. So more it be!

You should then spend a small amount of time at the altar, silently communing with the Dark Goddess, before burning the seal and going to bed.

To obtain love:

At its most basic, this seal exists to help in the recovery of a wandering lover, but it is regarded as being far more powerful than merely that. The seal defends love in all its forms, be it the love between a couple or the love within a family. It can even help a person suffering from self-doubt, which is nothing more than a lack of love for one's self.

The seal is created with symbols of love added to it that the adept finds the most personal. Those symbols could be in the shape of a heart, or they might involve a sketch of the Santa Muerte surrounded by a group of people who represent a family. Whatever imagery creates the feeling of the love that is lost, or is in danger of being lost, in your mind will work with this seal.

Having filled the two circles you should then write your petition to the Dark Goddess in red ink. Set out the case simply, and then fold your seal and hold it firmly to your breast.

Your conjuration should be along these lines:

Dark Mother of the day and the night: I conjure by the power of this seal so that you can feel my sadness and give me comfort. Restore to me the love that is lost. (Here you may very briefly state the facts of the matter.) So mote it be!

This is a very sentimental ritual, and one that you might want to take your time with. Sit at the altar and allow all your emotions to run free. You can repeat the conjuration if you wish, and then spend more time allowing your heart to open to the Dark Lady so that she may ease your pain.

When you are ready, then burn the seal before leaving the altar.

The Great Seal of Power:

This seal is considered to be the most powerful of them all. So potent is it that all the sources that were used for this book agree that it can only be used once every year - and a full year then needs to go by before it can be used again.

When used in conjunction with any other conjuration it will increase the energy generated and boost it enormously. For this reason alone, the Great Seal of Power should only be used for the most important rituals.

Many people recommend that the Great Seal should be created on the 31st December, with its conjuration being uttered as the New Year begins. That way the Great Seal will work throughout the coming months to increase the power of the adept's work.

The seal must include a drawing of the earth. I know that sounds difficult, but there are enough clipart images on the Web that you can download, print up and then trace if you get stuck.

Your petition should be written in green ink, and you are advised to concentrate on the matters that are the most important to you, rather than going for a broad approach that seeks everything. Use a spiritual rapier, in other words, rather than an axe.

Finally, the consensus of views that were sought for this book concluded that a suggestion as to the form of words that the invocation should take would be a bad idea. They have to come from you in every way. "From deep within your very soul," as one adept said.

Think carefully about the form of words that will encapsulate everything that your conjuration to the Santa Muerte should contain, and then speak them as the clock hits midnight and the New Year begins.

So mote it be!

Chapter Twelve

The Symbolism of the Coconut

The coconut has a special magical place in many cultures, and it has now been added to the Santa Muerte rites by many practitioners who use its water instead of the simpler kind from the tap.

The significance comes from the interior of the fruit, which is always white. Thus it relates directly to the soul, the thoughts and the positive desires of those who follow the Santa Muerte. Needless to say, it also relates to the spiritual purity that is to be found in every human.

The water inside the coconut is always fresh and pure by its very nature. That is why it is increasingly being used in all manner of Santa Muerte rituals, especially those which seek to combat negative energies that are trying to enter a house or person.

The hard brown casing represents the egoism and vanity that we humans sadly possess. The followers of the Santa Muerte who have adopted the coconut in their rituals believe that it represents their aim of striking though the hard, seemingly unyielding, outer casing that men and women carry about as part of their daily lives, to seek the pure, clean interior of their beings.

The Mexican adept who has spoken to this writer the most about this aspect of the Santa Muerte ritual said that her most important ritual involved the creation of a drink that was a fusion of the water and milk of the coconut. She makes the milk herself by grating the coconut flesh and then squeezing it through cheesecloth, but admitted that shop bought coconut milk that comes in a can would do at a pinch.

The amount of milk to coconut water is really a matter of personal taste, as is any addition of grated coconut to the liquid, so that can be left to the individual reader to decide what best suits their palate.

The ritual, as passed over a telephone line from Mexico, involves nothing more than creating a tall glass of coconut drink which is then placed in a bowl full of ice on the altar. The adept then sits quietly and meditates on the meaning of the Santa Muerte, and how she can improve her abilities in the service of the Dark Goddess.

When the drink is cold, she takes the glass in both hands and raises it in tribute to the Santa Muerte before drinking the cool, refreshing, pure liquid.

This practitioner reported that afterwards she felt refreshed, as if her body had been cleansed internally of many of the impurities that we humans pick up just by living in a modern, complex and frankly downright incoherent society.

Given that the whole of the Santa Muerte belief system is about making sense of a senseless world, many people will be able to understand her point and share it fully.

Chapter Thirteen

Some Final Thoughts

As part of my research for this booklet I spoke to at least a dozen followers of the Santa Muerte in Mexico City, many of them more than once. Most of what they told me is contained in the book that you have just read, but I do want to emphasise here that there was never any full agreement as to exactly how a ritual had to be performed. To make matters worse, when I turned to printed secondary sources things became even more confusing. Often one writer would say one thing, only to have his words contradicted by someone else in another work.

Making sense of the conflicting information seemed impossible, until I decided that I would give less weight to the published information, as it was probably written by people who were borrowing from each other and then adding bits on to make the books slightly more readable. That, or they were relying on just one or two informants within the craft.

I went back to the women that I had previously spoken to - and the bulk of my informants were women, something I will look at in more detail in a moment - to ask them about these seeming contradictions. The replies that I received were interesting, because instead of condemning my other sources as heretics, the women would often nod their heads and tell me that maybe the other woman knew something that they didn't. They would then adjust their own rituals to take into account the information that had just been passed to them.

Looking at my notes I then realised that the differences were really only ones of degree. Some people would emphasise one thing, whereas others would stress another, but they were all saying more or less the same thing, and aiming at identical ends.

It was at that moment that a light came on inside my head. I realised that the Santa Muerte is not just a folk religion, but it is a folk religion that is in the process of being formed right now. Followers of the Dark Lady are picking things up and trying them out, only to discard those which do not work very well in favour of rituals that do.

For the British person who is interested in the Santa Muerte and wants to begin practising the rites in this country, this is all very good news indeed. It means that you can borrow from others the things that work for them and add them to what you have learned in this book. I don't think that you should feel embarrassed by doing that in the slightest. After all, if the Santa Muerte worshippers in Mexico, the home of the religion, can take things from Catholicism, Santeria, and the various strands of Mexican witchcraft, the notion that you cannot borrow from the British Wicca is absurd.

Who knows? Perhaps in another generation, a young British woman who is as yet unborn may be invited to Mexico to be installed as the first High Priestess of the Santa Muerte Church. If that sounds fanciful, and I must admit that it does sound pretty fanciful to me, then who would have thought that just over twenty-five years ago a set of supernatural beliefs that were held by a few inhabitants of the Mexican slums would emerge as one of the fastest-growing religions in the world today?

That it will be a priestess, rather than a priest, strikes me on present trends to be pretty much axiomatic. That is not to say that men do not worship the Santa Muerte, because probably as many men hold her to their hearts as women, but the females do seem to be more involved with the rituals than the men.

Mexican men will wear a silver Santa Muerte belt buckle, or they will carry an image of the goddess in their wallets. Taxi drivers will often have a very small statuette on their dashboards, and men seem to be more likely than women to draw deeply on their cigarettes before blowing the smoke over the Santa Muerte as they ask her to bestow favours upon them.

However, when it comes to the full, ritual aspects of worship, doing something other than blowing smoke in other words, women outnumber men by rather a large percentage. For every man who has a tiny three inch statuette on his dashboard there are any number of women who perform serious rituals to try and ensure that all the drivers return home safe and sound at the end of the day.

The women that I spoke to tended to claim that the reason for this is that women are more spiritual than men, and gain comfort from the ritual aspects of their worship far more than men ever would.

I will leave you, the reader, to ponder on that if you wish, as my work here is almost complete.

Before I end this booklet, if any of you want to have a Santa Muerte statuette, either as the centrepiece of a new altar or as a conversation piece for your house, then Amazon UK and eBay both have sellers looking for your custom.

For my part, I have a stock of statuettes, incense sticks and small Santa Muerte cards that have an image of the goddess on one side and a conjuration - in Spanish, naturally - on the other. Please drop me a line to kennethcharlesbell@gmail.com if you want more details.

Lightning Source UK Ltd.
Milton Keynes UK
UKHW010646260919
350502UK00001B/71/P